I WAS only 23 when I first met Alex Mitche
Tintock Cup."

I began, with the arrogance of youth,
panto book by James Bridie (there's a cl

I wrote some bits and pieces myself,
journalist who could write scripts. That

Our fateful meeting over a cup of tea
in Sauchiehall Street led to his writing for that show and the two Citizens' pantos that followed.

Those pantos led to my doing a radio revue called "It's All Yours", and finally to the famous Five Past Eight shows.

So began a collaboration that has gone on for forty years.

His value to me as a script-writer is equalled only by my great affection for him as a man.

Gentle, urbane and gallant in a way that is considered old-fashioned, his clothes and manners are always just right and although slow to wrath, he is not unascerbic of tongue.

Even people he dislikes are never shown anger or discourtesy; in fact it's almost a weakness.

We'd spend hours preparing scripts in his Pollokshields home, sustained by his late wife Mary's wonderful free-range chicken-breast sandwiches.

Then agonising over its worth when it was written.

Fortunately Alex is an optimist, and I'm at the other end of the emotional spectrum, so we complemented each other well.

Suffice to say that of the material we didn't jettison, 90 per cent has provided me with quite memorable material. Lines that are remembered by audiences for many years.

Although his "Ballhead" and "Rosemary Gusher" are my own favourites, there's no doubt about the item that took Scotland by storm and has enjoyed great longevity —"Parliamo Glasgow."

This was ALL Alex. An exercise in ingenuity—the interplay of sound and sense manipulated by a superb juggler of language.

Your mastery of English has to equal your knowledge of the Glasgow argot. Alex certainly has both.

Now in his eighties, with eyesight not so good, he is indebted to his daughter, Jaye Maxwell, for typing these pieces. You'll enjoy them.

— Stanley Baxter

When There's A Royal Visit . . .

TWO archetypal Glasgow ladies, Mattie and Sadie, were in the enthusiastic crowd that welcomed the Queen to Glasgow for the formal inauguration of the Year of Culture.

A native word of commendation came from Mattie when Her Majesty appeared:

AWSHIZLUVLI!

Sadie agreed:

SOSHYIZ

Commenting on the Queen's purple coat, with hat to match, Mattie enthused with:

RAPURPLESUITSUR

Sadie wanted to know what places Her Majesty and the Duke of Edinburgh would visit. Mattie told her:

THURGAUNOANATOUR

Sadie asked her to elaborate:

TOUROWHIT?

Mattie revealed:

RACULCHURBITSORATOON

Sadie was aghast when informed that the Queen would visit an exhibition of modern art and exclaimed:

AHSEENIT!

"Did ye like it?" Mattie wanted to know. From Sadie, this brought an emphatic:

NAWAHDIDNI!

Which met with the traditional query:

HOWRAT?

Sadie dismissed the "controversial" art show with a scathing:

LOTAKIDMALEARI

The two ladies gravitated to George Square and the portals of the City Chambers.

They were impressed by the large number of people following the Royal pair into the Chambers. Sadie asked:

WHERRUREYGAUN?

Au fait with the Royal programme, Mattie informed her that the 600 or so guests were entertaining the Queen to an official banquet. Sadie was amazed:

AWTHEMYINS STUFFINTHURTURKIZ

Mattie had read in her paper that the banquet would include prawn cocktails and smoked salmon. She added:

ITLCOASTAMINT

"Hivvin help us!" shrilled Sadie, "Ah've jist:

PEYEDMAPOLLTAX

"And Ah'm gaun' hame tae:

MINCEANTOTTIZ"

Mattie was somewhat surprised at her friend's lack of culinary culture, and suggested she might use the mince to more exotic effect by making:

SPAGETTIBOLLYNEESY or LASANGY

Sadie ignored this slight on her homely kitchencraft, preferring to speculate on the table plan inside the City Chambers:

ZLIZGONNYSITWIRAELPEE?

Mattie, with her insider's knowledge of Royal protocol, was able to confirm that indeed, Her Majesty would dine with the Lord Provost. But she wondered:

WITKINSHI TOCKTAEHURABOOT?

Sadie, habituee of many a hen night, had no doubts about the course the conversation would take between the two ladies:

THULNATTERABOOT THURMENANTHURWEANS

On First Attending A Classical Concert

CULTURE-SEEKERS crowding into a classical concert might well include those native Glaswegians, Danny and Sadie.

English folk—and other foreign visitors—might be bewildered by the words and phrases used by the couple.

Sadie might comment on the audience:

SHOORA TOAFFINOSES

She realises that this is not the kind of concert she had thought it would be. She inquires of her husband:

WHITTUR WEDAENERE?

He replies that they are:

FURRABITTA CULCHUR

The orchestra starts to play a solemn piece. The lady is critical, and complains:

NOMUCHIACHUNE

Her husband informs her:

SBEET HOEVIN

His wife's attention wanders. She spots the cello player and directs her better half to:

LUKATRATWEESOWL WIRRABIGFIDDLE

Further, she goes as far as to suggest that:

EESHOULDSWOP

Which baffles Danny, who inquires:

WHIDJEMEANSWOP?

An impatient Sadie elucidates for his benefit:

SWOPRABIGFIDDLE FURRAURRAFELLASFLUTE

Feeling the conversation is veering somewhat from serious musical criticism, Danny essays a change in topic, opining that Beethoven's composition is:

NOBADFURRADEEFIE

Sadie misunderstands the reference to the composer's aural disability, replying:

MIBBYNO BUTAMNODEEF

Danny doesn't want to prolong such a ridiculous conversation. He whispers fiercely to her:

PIRRASOACKINIT

Sadie complies, but soon returns to the offensive. Indicating the gentleman with the baton, she inquiries:

HOOZATWIRAWEESTICK?

On being informed that he is the conductor, Sadie indulges in some witty audience participation by crying fortissimo:

HAWJIMMY GEEZWANTAERA GALLAGATE!

Danny is mortified by his partner's request for a bus ticket to the East End of Culture City. In an effort to remove her from the scene, he slips her a pound note, telling her to:

GAUNGETUZAKIAORA

It is some time before Sadie returns to her seat. She regretfully informs Danny she was unable to obtain a carton of orange juice, but announces gleefully that:

AHNIPTOOTFURRANIP

After what seems an eternity to Sadie, the concert comes to an end. She glares at her husband when he asserts:

RATWIZRERRMUSICWINTITNO?

But his wife's response is emphatic:

GIEMEJIMMISHANDOANITIME

Shopping At The Sales

WHATEVER time of year you choose to visit Glasgow, you'll want to leave yourself enough time to sample the wares in the city's stores.

Be sure the shops will be doing all they can to prise pennies from your purse—especially at sale time.

Whether you go bargain-hunting in summer or in January, you will experience yet more variations in vocabulary.

Under no circumstances venture forth without deep study of this glossary of words and phrases for indulging in the ancient Glaswegian rite of trekkinroonrasales:

HOODJI

That's a word frequently employed by those thrown off balance by over-enthusiastic fellow shoppers.

It occurs in such sentences as:

HOODJI HINK YURSHUVVIN?

Which translates as—"Would you kindly get your elbow out of my back?"

HOODJI LIKE WANOANADIAL?

Would you care to receive a smack on the mouth?

SOME equally interesting terms are used by ladies at the hat counter:

RATSMADAMPHAT

I intend to purchase that hat, madam.

AACHITS NOYUHEN

It's out of character with your personality.

OWHITTA BIGBAWFACE

That hat gives your face a rounded look.

SAMERCY YUVBIGLUGS

Were it not for your aural appendages, that hat would descend over your countenance.

TAKKITAFF AFOARA BURSTMASTEYS

Remove your headgear before it results in my sartorial disintegration.

ONE of the most frequently used words is AHINKUL, employed as follows:

AHINKUL GERRA FLERRED PERR IN LERRA FUR SERAH

I shall treat my daughter to a pair of flared, leather trousers.

Gentlemen accompanying wives at sales may be heard intoning traditional laments, like:

WHIDDIA WAANTWIA FLOORYSHURT?

I have no desire to attire myself like a surfer on Bondi Beach.

WIVGOARRA FRIANPANAREADI

Our kitchen is fully equipped.

SOME expressions heard at dress sales are sheer poetry:

RISFROAKWID GIEYE RABOAK

This creation is clearly not worth the price it bears.

YIDLUCKKAMESS INRATRIDDRESS

You would not appear at your best in that red creation.

Finally, there's the heart-rending call heard on all sides:

MARUDDISPUDS IZZAW SWALLTUP

I'm disturbed at how my pedal extremities have increased in size.

Happy hunting, folks.

A Tour Of The Barras

NOT all shopping has to be done in department stores, shopping malls or trendy city centre outlets.

Let us never forget that Glasgow has another world-famous shopping attraction—RABARRAS.

This is not, as one might imagine, a romantic Far Eastern city. It is a collection of stalls from which are sold:

RERBARGINS

The vendors who sell a variety of goods from the stalls are known as:

BARRABOYS

To attract customers to his stall, one such vendor may offer an article at a remarkably low price. He invites prospective buyers to:

ROLLUPNOO

As curious prospective buyers flock to the stall, the salesman addresses a lady in the forefront of the crowd. He inquires of her:

WANNABURGINHEN?

He holds up a china teapot and informs her:

AHMGIENITAWA

The lady is obviously making up her mind whether or not to take the teapot. The vendor cajoles her with:

GENYINEWEDGEWOODBEN

Another lady gives her opinion of the stallholder:

APROAPURFLYMAN

The lady and her daughter move on to another stall. Suddenly the daughter cries:

OMAW LUKATRAT!

This vendor is holding up what he describes as a:

RALESILKHEIDSCARF

The young lady says she'd like to buy it. She repeats:

RALESILK!

Her mother doesn't agree. Emphatically she declares:

RALESILKMAFIT SJISTADAUDAPOLYESTER

Mother and daughter move on to yet another stall. At this one, a vociferous gent is endeavouring to sell fruit. He bellows:

LUVLISEVILLOARINGES

And he adds:

NANEOYUR FURRINRUBBISH!

Not taken in by the claim that citrus fruit grows in the Clyde Valley, our intrepid bargain hunters take their custom elsewhere. They find themselves being urged to buy:

OFFEESHELSATLITEDISHES

Keen to sample the delights of extra-terrestrial television, daughter has a closer look at the dishes. Then she exclaims:

SARIDDYBINLIDPENTITWHITE!

The stall-holder is offended by this perceptive remark and informs the young lady she would be well advised to:

ZIPYERLIPYAHERRY

Unwilling to make the acquaintance of the ape-like gentlemen emerging from behind the stall, the pair take flight to the nearby bistro, "Sam 'n' Ella's." Daughter inquires of her mother:

JIWAANTATOTTISCOAN?

Rather disillusioned by her recent experience, mother replies in a sullen tone:

DITFAWAFFRABACKOA TOTTISCOANLORRY?

Unfortunately, she is overheard by a passing waitress who rounds off a perfect day by informing her that she is a:

TORNFACEDAULBIZZUM

Attending A Cocktail Party

THERE will be an endless round of social events for the culture vultures throughout the year.

Many will take the form of a cocktail party, a cheese-and-wine or something similarly formal.

Some visitors might even attain the dizzy social heights of a civic reception.

Whatever the circumstances, there will be a certain pattern to the proceedings, and predictable behaviour from some who might not be totally prepared.

For a start, they will encounter a distinctive dialect known as POASHTALK.

It distinguishes the speech of certain residents in the city's exclusive suburbs.

Elistair will greet Ian with "How are you?" It has a distinctly Japanese sound:

HOWAYU?

The answer to that question seldom varies:

NOTOOBED HOWAYEW?

Their hostess approaches with a tray of drinks. She asks:

ANOTHAH CHAIRRIBRENDY ELISTAIR?

Elistair takes the glass and expresses his gratitude with a typical poashtalk word:

THENKSAWFLY

Ian refuses a refreshment and tells the hostess:

NOTFAWME ENGELA

A reply that shocks Angie into asking:

WHA!NUT?

And Ian has to explain that the breathalyser is in the back of his mind:

ECTWALLEH AIMDRAIVING

JAKE and his wife, Jinty, on the other hand, are first-timers to the cocktail circuit.

Jake surveys the buffet table, with dainty delicacies laid thereupon, and comments:

SASWELLWIVETT

But despite declaring that he has enjoyed his normal repast before attending, he hungrily reviews the range of vol-au-vents:

YONWEEPIESUVNAELIDS

He is unimpressed by their size, and declares he will eat them:

TWATTATIME

He doesn't rate the quality of the chicken, either, claiming it's:

OFFYRUBBRY

The whole set-up prompts him to reflect on the fact the tickets were £15 each:

RUDDIRIPAFF

THE party ends at a late hour.

Wee Maisie, the maid, has had a busy evening washing glasses and carrying plates of canapes.

As the guests leave she watches from the front door. She pronounces her verdict on them with a phrase beginning with the word ASHOORA:

ASHOORA SNOTTICHANCERS

Later, telling her mother of the evening's proceedings, she refers to the guests and their cars:

RAWIFESDONERADRIVIN

And she makes a serious allegation—that the husband of each lady had:

ARICHTGUIDBUCKITOANIM

Standing In The Chip Shop Queue

IF the cocktail party has left the guests feeling that something more substantial by way of sustenance is required, they might be attracted by the tempting, irresistible aroma coming from one of the city's many traditional ethnic eating houses—the chipper!

Wherein they will almost certainly be priviliged to hear distinctive dialogue, not used in any other place in the world, let alone the European City of Culture.

In the queue at the counter are Sue and Paula. Sue says she is extremely hungry and gives the reason for this:

AMFAMISHT ADNAEDENNER

Paula observes that they are about to be served by the young lady behind the counter who demands to know:

WHITYOOZFUR?

Sue cannot decide. She scans the menu and is urged on by the assistant who snaps out the word:

GERRAJILDYOAN MAKUPYERMIN'

Sue eventually reaches a decision:

ONYPUDDENS?

There has been great demand for the batter-covered oatmeal delicacies. She's told:

WIRRASELTOOTAPUDDENS

With a shrug of acceptance, both girls settle for something less exotic:

PITISINAHADDOCK

To establish whether or not they wish the order to be accompanied by French fries, the assistant enquires tactfully:

ZATTASINGULORASUPPIR?

To a sizzling accompaniment from the deep friers, the assistant gently solicits information as to whether or not the girls wish to take advantage of accompanying condiments, provided free of charge:

SALTENVINGIR?

Paula nods her assent, and scans the counter until her eyes settle on additional options. Whereupon she intones:

GIESADAUDOHP

With the battered fish and French fries liberally sprinkled with a layer of salt, dripping vinegar and layered with the brown substance from the bottle on the counter, Sue says:

AWFFYWATTERYSAS

Ignoring the criticism of that particular spice's viscosity, the serving wench has only one additional question:

DUBBLERAPT?

Since the girls are desirous of taking their meal home before partaking of it, they take advantage of this generous offer of free gift paper.

Paula has one last request before the sports pages are quickly turned in under the parcel:

SEESTWAINGINSTAE

Thus, within minutes, another two Glasgow gourmets leave the premises as satisfied customers. Or are they?

As Sue leaves the shop, she says to a stranger in the queue:

SNAWFYPRICENOO

She thereby risks the stranger making a comparison with bygone days when the same premises were run by a swarthy, moustachioed gentleman who spoka witha di accent thata suggested hissa roots were inna Roma rather than Rutherglen:

ANSNOASGUIDASRATALLIES:

But the stranger is nothing if not a patriot. His parting shot reveals clearly that he still prefers his haddock and chips to anything he might be served with in the Tandoori establishment further down the street:

BETTIRANNABUNA

Joining The Tartan Army

IT'S likely some visitors to Glasgow this summer will move on to Italy for the World Cup finals. It's even more likely they will find themselves in the company of Scottish supporters.

Until that moment, they might have deluded themselves that they understood English! They will soon learn otherwise.

On their arrival in Genoa, the Scottish fans will raise their voices in various traditional carnival cries. Such as:

AKID DAEWIAPIE

Which translates as "I am desirous of consuming our national dish."

JINGSAVATHURST

I am in dire need of liquid refreshment.

WHERRABAUR?

Where may I quench my thirst?

CANNYSEE NAEPUB!

There appears to be a distinct dearth of public houses.

HOFFANNA HOFPAL

Kindly supply me with a whisky and a beer.

GOARAVBIN STUNG!

The refreshments are even more expensive than in Scotland!

AS they wait in the stadium for the game to begin, Scots fans may make remarks like these:

TAKYURHOARN OOTMALUG

I say, old chap, be good enough to blow your trumpet in a different direction.

ZARRAGUY FRAERAGODFAITHER?

Have I not seen that uniformed gentleman on television?

NAW, SAFUNNYPOLIS

No, he is a native policeman.

LOOKOWRERR ERRANDY!

The Scottish team manager has arrived.

ANDIEZNO BOATHURT

Mr Roxburgh is preserving his customary equanimity.

WHEN the games against Costa Rica, Sweden and Brazil begin, the Scottish fans will start to give vent to a constant stream of picturesque comments:

ARRABOYALLY!

Let us revel in the expertise of Mr McCoist.

ZATNOA RERRPASS!

The accuracy of our sweeper, Mr McLeish, is most pleasing.

HAWRERR RATSAFOUL!

That was an extremely late tackle by the opposing centre-back.

GETRATREFAPERRASPECS

I am positive that the referee has mislaid his glasses.

BLINZABAT

I am still concerned over the referee's eyesight!

ACHPIRRIM AFFRAPARK!

That player might have been given a custodial sentence had his offence been committed on the streets.

IF Scotland lose, the air will be rent with such age-old Caledonian laments as:

SADAMPTSWINL or
WEWUZ ROABBED

But if Scotland win, the streets of Genoa will resound to the **WIRRA** cry:

WIRRA TEAM!
WIRRA GEMME!
WIRRADAY FURSCOA'LAN!

Plane Speaking!

IT is just possible that before they leave for Italy, the intrepid travellers might experience a slight delay at the airport.

Believe it or not, such things have been known to happen.

As a consequence of which, it is best to be prepared for the lingo of the lounge!

After waiting five hours for a plane to Benidorm, Teenie might put the blame on European air traffic controllers, observing:

SRAERUDDIFURRINURS

Tommy, her husband, expresses regret that they hadn't decided to spend their holiday nearer at hand, perhaps down the Clyde coast. He growls:

SHOULDAWENTIROASSI

A small individual, an airport employee, passes by. Tommy detains him and asks:

WHIRRABOOTOORPLANE?

The small gent replies rather curtly:

DOANASKME ADOANNO

Teenie is annoyed and calls the man an:

IMPIDDINTWEENYAFF

(It should be explained here that the term NYAFF is applied only to small males. The expression BIG NYAFF is never used. A large gent who is unduly aggressive is called a BIG NYUCK.)

Tommy suggests they give up waiting and states that they can:

CUMBACKRAMORRA

His wife rejects that proposal with an emphatic:

NAWWULLNO

Then she tries to make conversation. She tells her husband:

FLOZFLEWTIFLORIDA

Teenie gives more information pertaining to Florence's vacation in America:

GAUNTAEDISNEYLAUN

All her husband says about this is that it will be a:

CHEENGEFAEBARRALAN'

Standing In The Bus Queue

TRAVELLING by public transport will greatly enrich the vocabulary of the visitor.

At one of the city's thousands of bus stops, a lady might be heard to complain that she has been waiting for a bus for:

MERRNHOFFANOOR

Commenting further on this disgraceful state of affairs, another lady uses the well-known Glaswegian word SADAMPT in her protest:

SADAMPT DISGRACE

SADAMPT is used in other stern criticism, such as:

SADAMPT SHAME, SADAMPT RIPAFF, SADAMPT LIBBURTY

The seeker after culture will no doubt want to visit the Burrell Collection on the South side of the city. If he or she asks someone in the queue how to get there, the information may be puzzling:

TWINNYWANTAERASHAWS

Which means simply "A number Twenty-Ŏne bus to Pollokshaws".

As often as not, someone else in the queue will intervene with the suggestion:

TAKKATAXI

And will further explain:

CHEAPURFURRABUNCHAYIZ

One lady expresses a fear that the bus timetable has been altered and the bus they are waiting for may not appear. She says pessimistically:

MIBBITHUVTOOKITAFF

Another lady gives vent to a cry of despair. She repeats the Slavonic-sounding TOOKITAFF in the sentence:

SHAIRLYITSNOBIN TOOKITAFF

An elderly gentleman in the queue takes a philosophical view of the situation and expresses himself in two picturesque words:

WELHUVTIHOOFIT INTIRATOON

Making Use Of Public Transport

THE native patois is heard at its most charming once you're aboard the city's double-decker buses.

And the experience will almost certainly start when the vehicle comes into view.

Its arrival will bring the comment:

HEREZWANOO

Which is usually followed by the remark:

NUTTAFORETIME

The driver, who also takes the fares, informs his latest passenger:

FOOUPINSIDE

And he directs the newcomer to the top deck with:

SATESOANTOAP

A stout lady making her way to the top deck by the precipitous spiral stairway may exclaim:

GOAASHAMSTUCK!

She will then request the person behind her to:

GEEZAPUNTUP

On reaching the top deck, the stout lady espies an acquaintance, a younger lady with a baby in her lap.

The stout lady sits down beside her and asks the young mother:

ZISYURYOUNGES'?

Told that he is indeed the youngest of the family, the stout lady wants to know:

IZZITALKINYIT?

The young mother replies with "Aye", and urges the baby to:

SAYSOMETHINTAERALADY

The child surveys the large lady and says:

AWANGITWAASHED.

She is impressed, and exclaims:

OHMEH! WHITTALUVLY CLEARSPEAKUR

MEANWHILE, downstairs, a brouhaha is in the making. A young man with closely-cropped hair and a penchant for tattoos has lit a cigarette in defiance of local statutes.

An elderly gent behind him exhorts him to:

PITITOOTYESCUNNER

The shaven-headed youth is no respecter of age and replies:

TOCKINTAEMEHUMPHY?

The elderly gent is affronted. He informs the illegal smoker that:

AFOTAWARFURRALIKESAYOU

By now the lower deck is in uproar. The bus stops and the driver storms up to the scene of the commotion. He delivers an ultimatum to the youth:

RAFAGSOOTURYOOROOT

The youth stubs the offending weed on the floor and mutters one damning word:

PERRABAMS

Just A Day's Shopping . . .

SHOPPING in the city centre can be an experience—and an education—provided you take this crash course in the appropriate terminology:

For instance, two young ladies Michelle and Karen are lingering at the clothes counter. Once again Michelle uses the interesting word AHINKUL. This denotes a certain measure of indecision. She tells her chum:

AHINKULGOFURRAMINI

Karen delicately points out that Michelle's lower limbs are not exactly ideal for the wearing of a mini-skirt.

She hints that her friend has a tendency to be bow-legged. She says falteringly:

NORATYURAWFYBOWLLYBUT

The two damsels drift over to the dress counter where Karen picks up a gown and holds it against herself.

As she seeks Michelle's opinion, she employs another picturesque phrase:

JEHINKUL SUITRISFROACK?

Michelle is not over-enthusiastic about the suitability of the dress. She thinks it is too small and tells her friend:

SOFFISKIMPIOANYE!

OVER in the menswear department, a woman points out an attractive garment to her husband:

ERRARERRSHURT

The gent doesn't agree with her. He says, "A purple shirt wi' green stars on it?" And adds:

WERRATHING? AMNOGLAIKIT!

He is appalled when his wife suggests that he buy a suit at £100. He protests that he is not a millionaire:

JITHINKAM HINGINWIDOUGH?

His wife insists he is badly in need of new clothing as his appearance is so shabby. She likens him to something that has:

FELLAFFAFLITTIN

Resentful of this description, the gentleman blasts back:

YIRNOMAKKINME INTIATOAFF

"Naw", says the wife, and adds:

AMNOA RUDDIWIZARD

THE shop assistants themselves have a quaint turn of phrase that takes some getting used to. The following expressions are in common usage:

WURRA SELTOOTARAT

Which indicates the article you desire is no longer in stock.

AVNO TWAPERRAHONZ

I am not physically equipped to serve more than one person at a time.

YIZL HUVTICUE

I would be obliged if you ladies would wait in turn.

GOATNUHINWEEIR?

Have you nothing less than a £20 note?

SWENTUP

The cost of that particular item has increased since last you visited the store.

SMATEEBREKNOO

I regret I cannot serve you at the moment. I am about to partake of a refreshing cup of Darjeeling.

TOOWEEFUR YURBAHOOCHY

I am afraid madam will need a larger hip size.

A Word About The Weather

MAJOR recurring topic of conversation in Scotland is the weather.

Be it fair or foul, the terms used to describe it can be baffling in the extreme.

Further study of Glesceranto is needed if you are to fully understand matters of meteorological importance.

SNOABAD DAYRADAY

An indication that the weather has been worse.

RISWERRA WIDSCUNNURYE

I am displeased with the climatic conditions.

SANGAVA KOLRADAY

I am glad I did not dispense with my semmit.

These, of course, are general descriptions to be exchanged on first meeting any visitor. There are more pointed phrases, viz:

RASUNZOOT

The sun is shining.

MADIALZBEALIN

The sun has had an adverse effect on my complexion.

MASHURTS STIKKINTIMME

The heat is causing me sartorial inconvenience.

NOTICE how few phrases there are to describe a sunny day. The list for rainy days is rather longer:

SGONNICUMDOON

The low cloud ceiling would indicate rain is imminent.

ZARRASPITTARAIN?

Is it about to rain?

ERRARAAINOANNOO

Yes, it's just started raining.

SCUMMINDOONIN KATZINDOAGS

It's a cloudburst.

SOANFURRADAY

The downpour is likely to be protracted.

GERRINTYRATCLOSE

Let us quickly seek shelter in that entry;

SHOODABRUNG WURWELLIZ

We should have equipped ourselves with water-resistant footwear.

ERRABLINKABLUE!

I discern a break in the clouds.

RAINSWENTAFF

The downpour has abated.

RATWINDSA PEST

The gale that has sprung up is disconcerting.

AMCHITRINWIRRACOL

The temperature is causing me to shiver.

BELLAZBROLLIZBLEWOOT

Bella's umbrella has been rendered useless by the wind.

WISHTAD BEDATHAME

I'm so disillusioned with the weather I wish I hadn't ventured out.

AMFROZE TAERAMARRA

The temperature is extremely low.

AFELTANNURRA SPOATTHERR

It's about to rain again.

SOANAGAIN WORSER

This downpour is even heavier than before.

Lastly, we leave you with a typical native wish for your holidays:

BERRA WERRA FURRA FERR!

If You Need A Doctor

THE possibility of the visitor having to visit a doctor cannot be ruled out. Whilst words like OXTER, PEELY-WALLY and SCUNNERED now have almost universal usage, some other expressions are just a shade more baffling.

A study of the following list will greatly assist in understanding ailments that frequently afflict Glaswegians:

SAWSWALTUPDOAC

Note the acute swelling doctor.

SELLUVASERRTAE

It is also extremely painful.

AMAFFMACHUCK

My appetite is poor.

VANOFFISERRKYTE

I'm suffering from stomach pains.

MANOAZISFERSTAPPIT

My nasal passages are blocked.

AMBAKWIMMABAK

Once again I have a sore back.

MAFITZLOUPIN

I should never have worn those platform shoes.

MAHEIDSAYERR

I have frequent headaches.

AMSEEKOAWRAPEELS

Surely, doctor, you aren't going to prescribe more tablets?

WHIRRABOORRABO'AL?

Could I have one of your pleasant-tasting prescriptions, please?

GONNIGEEZALINE?

I could do with a week in bed in this awful weather.

Overheard At The Laundrette

PERHAPS it will never have the atmosphere of the old steamie, but the laundrette still has a language all its own:

As Mattie enters with a loaded pram, her friend Millie remarks:

ZISSYOUHERE AGAIN?

Mattie explains why she is such a frequent attender at the laundrette.

She reminds Millie that she has:

FOWERWEANS ANAMANANALUDGER

Millie complains that her husband likes to change into fresh underwear frequently.

She is revolted by the very sight of his underpants and states she is:

SEECKORASICHTOLONGJOHNS

Mattie, too, resents having to spend so much time in the laundrette.

She informs Millie she'd prefer to watch *Take The High Road* rather than look at:

CLAESBIRLINROON

Millie is intrigued by a voluminous garment in her friend's washing.

She surmises that it is underwear belonging to Mattie's husband, and inquires:

ZATYURMANSIMMIT?

Mattie informs her that the large garment is in fact a jumper which she is washing for her daughter. She replies:

NAWSJENNIZJUMPUR

From the size of the jumper, Millie deduces that the daughter has put on weight.

She uses the ancient word HUZNIHOF in the observation:

SHEHUZNIHOFGREW

Mattie, resenting having to wash the jumper in the first place, adds:

SHIZGREWINTAEAPEST!

Near The Supermarket Checkout

NOT all the visitors' shopping will be done in city centre department stores.

Almost certainly at some stage they will find the need to avail themselves of the facilities of the friendly, neighbourhood supermarket.

And as they approach the check-out, they are liable to hear something along these lines:

Sadie is just behind Mattie in the checkout queue. She remarks that Mattie's basket is full to the brim.

Mattie uses the obscure word HINGINAFF to describe the strain of carrying her loaded basket:

MAERMSHINGINAFFME

She also discloses that walking round the supermarket has caused her feet to ache.

Again she uses HINGINAFF

MASPUDSISHINGINAFFME

Mattie then espies a lady writing busily at the checkout counter.

She recognises her as a neighbour who puts on airs. She names her thus:

BIGTEENIETOAFFINOSE

She further alleges that the lady is conceited, translating this into her native dialect as:

SHEFANCISHURBARRA

"She's peyin' fur hur messidges wi' a cheque!" cries Sadie.

Mattie is appalled at what she considers to be a piece of showing-off and calls:

SWANKINSCUNNER!

The cheque-signing lady responds with a phrase from another dialect heard in the City of Culture:

AIVA MAINDTOSLEPYOU

Mattie then threatens to give the uppity lady a blow on the mouth.

She uses the word WANOANRA in the sinister-sounding sentence:

ALGIEYE WANOANRAGUB

When Mattie reaches the checkout counter she finds to her dismay that she doesn't have enough cash to pay for the contents of her basket.

She turns to Sadie for help using the word GONNIGEESE.

She asks Sadie to lend her £1, saying:

GONNIGEESE ALENNIAWAANCER?

GONNIGEESE may also be used by the young supermarket assistant requesting a kiss from the girl he fancies at the cheese counter.

When they meet behind the packets of cereal, he might risk:

GONNIGEESE AWEECHEEPUR?

So Mattie and Sadie go their separate ways with the traditional phrases:

SEEYIRAMORRA and TERRARANOO

A Day On The Beach

WHILE Spanish hotel owners lament the decrease in the numbers of British holiday-makers, hundreds of citizens from the City of Culture will spend a day at Scottish resorts.

Visitors might care to join them on those safaris to the seaside.

By car, bus and train, many families will go:

AWAFURRADAY DOONTITROON

Happy hordes descend on the beaches of Ayrshire, and on all sides are heard the native greetings:

HULLAWRERR! or OSHURSEL!

Let us examine some of the words and phrases heard in the conversation of two middle-aged ladies, Sadie and Mattie as they recline on the sand dunes and survey other members of the bus party.

A young lady in a bikini passes by. Sadie identifies her as Michelle, daughter of Bella McGuffie. Mattie praises the maiden:

NICEFACE . . . . . NICEFIGGIR

But Sadie is critical of Miss McGuffie's nether limbs and adds:

PEETISHIZBOWLLY

Mattie is now peering, puzzled, into the middle distance. She asks her friend:

ZARRA STRANDITWHALE OWRERR?

Sadie reassures her:

NAW SPIGMISSUSBROON SUNBATHIN

The large lady also comes in for criticism, this time for her rearward dimensions:

SUMBAHOOCKEY OANUR

FURTHER down the beach, Wullie seeks a vacant deckchair for his wife, Winnie:

ERZWANER

His joy is short-lived when an alert attendant explains the cost of the hire:

PUNANOOR

Off they stomp, settling instead for a sunny spot amongst the dunes.

Wullie perks up when he espies a young lady who has braved the breeze and courageously set a topless trend:

WIDYELUKATTAT

Winnie does so, then renders a stern admonition:

IZEAFF

They have an hour in the sun before Winnie produces a flask of tea, crisps and filled rolls. Wullie's first bite prompts the age-old complaint at beach parties:

SANNIESAWSAUN

Still, he grinds his way through the mixture of meat paste, sauce and sand before Winnie, gazing out to sea, issues the ultimate challenge:

URYIGAUNINURNO?

Wullie is horrified at the prospect of having to paddle, let along immerse his ample girth in the sea. He uses the classic excuse:

FURGOTMATOOL

Winnie is not to be denied the opportunity to call his bluff of the previous evening:

YASEYERSEMMIT

Wullie plays his ace:

TIDEZOOT

So they snooze under the sun in silence until it gets too hot. Winnie comments that her spouse appears to be perspiring somewhat. He has his own succinct way of putting it:

SRUNNINAFFIZ

The Japanese Connection

NOT so long ago, a guide-book was published in Japanese. It was entitled "Glasgow - Your Ideal Holiday Centre" and was aimed primarily at the increasing number of Japanese businessmen and tourists.

An admirable gesture. But the authorities seemed to have overlooked the fact that many Japanese words and phrases were already in common use by the natives of Glasgow.

Since there is likely to be a considerable influx of camera-clad visitors from the Land of the Rising Sun this summer, it is appropriate to study again this Glasjapwegian glossary:

The most common is the friendly greeting:

HEYHU or HIYU

Other greetings refer to the weather:

OSAN OFFIDAI

Indicating that the weather is inclement.

OBI JINGSAMKOL

Reveals that the subject's body temperature is low.

Children also reveal obvious Oriental links, particularly with any invitation that includes the familiar WANNASUKAT:

WANNASUKAT MAOARINGE? or WANNASUKATMAJOOSE?

Other expressions with an Oriental connotation are likely to be heard in places as diverse as a doctor's to a dance hall:

GONNIGEISHA SANG?

Which means, "Kindly favour us with a ballad."

WHITWUNNA THREETHURTI?

Is a request for the name of the horse that came first past the post in the 3.30 pm race at Ayr.

OMATUMMI

I am assailed by stomach pains.

TWIZZAT HOATPI

The microwaved meat delicacy you consumed has given you indigestion.

OFFMAFITYU!

Expression used by a young lady to a clumsy dance partner.

IN the hostelries of the city, Japanese visitors may be surprised to hear many words of their own language being spoken. Thus we have:

TAKYA HAUFNU

Down your drink!

WISSAMARA WIYI?

Why is your walk so unsteady?

GOSHIZ BUNG FU!

The gentleman has wined rather too well.

HARIKARI RAKERI-OOT

A request for Harry to transport certain liquid assets.

OSHIZA WEEBRAMA

The barmaid is extremely attractive.

SOSHI IZ

I agree.

EVEN at the Yuletide season, remarks may be overheard that suggest they owe their origins to Tokio rather than Torryglen:

RATSA SNAWOAN-NU

We will have a white Christmas.

SANGAVA SLUSHI

Christmas in the city is not white after all.

THURRAHOLINASOLE OMAWELLI

My footwear is not suitable for this weather.

And when visitors from Japan leave for home, there will be familiar expressions ringing in their ears:

ORRABESTYA...TATARUNU!

The Holiday Photographs

VISITORS who are lucky enough to be guests of Glasgow families after the holidays will be in for a rare treat—the ceremonial showing of the snaps!

Glasgow folk use a language of their own when proudly displaying the artistry of their camera work.

Here are a few of these photographic phrases and their meanings:-

WANNYSEE WURPHOTIES?

Which is a warning to prepare yourself for an hour of utter boredom.

RATSMURRA PADDLIN

This first snapshot shows mother in an undignified posture, bathing her feet.

SHOULDNYA TOOKRAT

In this similar shot, mother is shaking her fist, protesting at having been photographed.

WEEFELLA BELLAFELLINWI

A diminutive gentleman who made the acquaintance of Bella.

ERRAT AULSCUNNER

This is a portrait of our landlady.

WIDGIE LOOKAT ROLYIN

Observe Grandfather's open mouth as he sleeps in a deck-chair.

ATTAKA NOFFIPHOTY

Photographs never flatter me.

AMAZFATTAZAT?

Am I as out of shape as the camera suggests?

BIGBABSBAKIN OANRABEACH

No, not a stranded whale, but Barbara sunbathing.

BOABHUNTIN FURRIZ WALLIZ

Robert hunting for his false teeth after an unfortunate mishap at the swimming pool.

RAWEAN FLINGIN SAUN

The child merrily scattering half the beach over everything and everyone in sight.

MAMAN SKELPIN RAWEAN

Father cutting short the child's enjoyment.

WHOZARRAGAIN?

I have forgotten the identity of that young lady.

SABURD SAMMYFELLOOTWI

It is the young lady cousin Sammy spent much of his holiday cash on.

OTHERRAPICNIC

Here is a group photograph of the family's al fresco party.

MAMAW YELLINUR HEIDAFF

Taken after mother inadvertently sat upon a wasp.

POLLIZ PEELLIWALLIWILLI

Polly's husband, William, after coming off the Big Dipper at Blackpool.

OF course there are times when a holiday snapshot doesn't quite come up to standard. On those occasions we are apt to hear the phrases:

MANTY SATOANMA KODAK

My aunt failed to notice the camera on the chair.

WURHEIDZIZCUTAFF!

Uncle Hughie had had a few refreshments before taking this photograph.

Orrabest, and always remember, watchraburdichinas!

For Youngsters At A Pop Concert

YOUNG visitors to the Cultural City will no doubt extend their quest for culture by attending a pop concert.

The language used by Marie and her "lumbur" (boyfriend) Boab, who might be seated nearby, will be baffling.

Boab is somewhat discomfited when he considers the price he has paid for two tickets. He muses:

TWINTIQUIDAPERR

His young lady seeks to console him and points out:

RAGROUPSBIGSTAURS

And she adds for emphasis:

TOAPARACHERTS

But Boab still considers the admission price is rather expensive. He goes on:

NAEWUNNER THURMILLIONERRS

But he approves of the group's opening number. He explains:

DEIDFUNKI!

The lead singer comes to the microphone for the next number.

It is Marie's turn to demonstrate enthusiasm. In a high-pitched wail she observes:

AWEEZGORJUSS!

Boab disapproves of this display of feeling. He criticises the appearance of the singer. He alleges that he has:

GOARRA BIGBAWFACE

When the song is over, Marie applauds wildly and squeals loudly. She tells her escort:

THATWIZMAAGIC!

She squeals again. Boab asks her why. She replies:

AMRATEXCITIT!

The young gent tells her that he had mistakenly thought she had severe stomach ache. Or, as he puts it:

APAININYURPEENY

THE concert goes on and Marie's enthusiasm is unabated. Her hand-clapping becomes more frenzied and her screams louder. Boab requests her to restrain herself:

GIEYURMOOTHAREST

Suddenly Marie tells Boab:

MAERMZIZSERR

Again comes that one-word request for information. Bob inquires:

HOWRAT?

His girl-friend enlightens him:

ERMZIZSERR CLAPPINMAHAUNSABOVEMAHEID

The concert ends. On the way out of the hall, Marie invites Boab back to her home. Yet again, his one-word qucry:

WHITFUR?

Marie drops the bombshell:

TAELETYEHEAR RAGROUPSTENSINGULS

Boab then addresses her with the picturesque word YURAFFYUR:

YURAFFYURCHUMP

In A Yuppie Wine Bar

IN recent years, more and more wine bars have been opened throughout Culture City.

They are patronised for the most part by young men in suits and old school ties, chaps whose homes are in the leafy suburbs.

Scots yuppies usually accompany chic young damsels.

The dialect-speaking Glaswegian rarely visits a wine bar.

When he does, he usually speaks out of the side of his mouth. To the young lady who has inveigled him into taking her to one of these places he may say:

SUMDUMPRIS FUACHANCERS

His fair companion may object to this complaint and say:

STOAPMUMPIN'

She will follow this with the request

LETSGERRA GLESSAWINE

Her escort asks if she is not having her usual refreshment:

URYENOFURRAVOADKA?

The young lady tells him firmly:

GETSA GLESSAWINE

Her companion, surprised, remarks:

YEWAANT RAMAMMIMINE?

"It's whit they huv here," the damsel tells him. "Whit ur YOU huvvin'?"

Her escort swiftly replies:

AHMFURRA HOFANAHOF

The young lady then warns him:

YURGONNIGIEME ARIDNECK

Before he can give his order, a yuppie brushes past him and calls imperiously to the barman:

TWOGLAHSSES OF RAIDWAIN

As the yuppie takes the two glasses of Beaujolais and goes off to rejoin his lady friend, the dissatisifed customer observes:

HIMANHURZOANRARIDBIDDI

The young lady remonstrates with her partner, informing him he is far too uncouth for such a cultured city:

YIRACOAMINWEENYAFF

Mr Glesca does not agree, and reminds the young lady that she was not always as cultured herself:

AKENTYEWEN YEDRANKBLACKANTANS

Deciding to turn the other cheek rather than cause a scene, she orders her partner's drink herself, asking the barman to:

GEEZAWEEPERRYHAY

On being confronted with a delicate glass of French mineral water, complete with slice of lemon, he sniffs then has a small sip. He explodes:

GIDGOADITSWAATER!

He then takes his fair companion by the arm and propels her to the exit door. The damsel asks:

WHAURURWEGAUN?

Promptly comes the reply:

TAEARERRWEEBOOZER

If You're Having A Refreshment

A SPECIAL sub-culture exists within Glasgow's many hostelries.

Since it's highly likely that visitors will seek to quaff an ale or two in the city's salubrious pubs, or perchance go upmarket and sip a G-and-T in a trendy wine bar or hotel lounge, it's vital they should acquaint themselves with the drinking dialogue.

It will stand them in equally good stead should they ever encounter Glaswegians on holiday. Because whether you meet them in Madrid or Musselburgh, one aspect of their enjoyment will never vary—the appreciation of a bar, bistro or bodega.

In the hope of lessening linguistic chaos, here's the offishul list of the more obscure words and phrases liable to be used by Glasgow boozers:

AMOANA

Is used in such phrases as AMOANABELL (I shall bear the expense of the company's libations) and AMOANAWAGGON (my digestion has become impaired by over-indulgence in cheap sherry).

URYEFURRANURRA?

This is the most common of several terms all meaning—"Are you capable of consuming yet another refreshment?"

Variations include "Whityefur?" and "Smaroon."

HEEZUDDANUFF

An expression generally used by a lady to indicate her husband is in imminent danger of falling flat on his back.

ALUVVA or YULUVVA

As in "Aluvva nurra Bacardi" and "Yuluvva serrheid ramorra."

WHERRJE PIRRITAW?

Can you explain your remarkable expertise in imbibing such a large quantity of liquid sustenance?

GOADAMDRY or AVVADROUTHOAN

Both signify the speaker is in dire need of an instant thirst-remover.

FURSTRADAY!

At home, I don't usually start drinking at 9 am.

HUVYONI?

Frequently heard in such questions as "Huvyoni pies?" . . . . . . "Huvyoni fags?" . . . "Huvyoni bigger glesses?"

RANYAFFS JAKED or RASCUNNURS STOCIOUS

That objectionable individual has had more than a modicum of intoxicating liquor.

HAWWULLIE SINGZASANG!

Let us induce William to provide vocal entertainment.

Finally, you must accept that you will NEVER hear the exclamation "Cheers" from any native of Glasgow, except perhaps select citizens of Mulguy.

They say farewell in that ancient Cowcaddens cry—

ORRARUDDYBEST FURRAFERRMAC!

Dining In A Small Cafe

THE easy informality of the waitresses is a delightful feature of some Glasgow cafes.

As a young couple seat themselves and are about to order a meal the waitress will ask:

WHITYIZWAANT?

The young gent will then turn to his lady friend to learn her choice.

He employs the oft-used Glaswegian inquiry:

WHITTURYEFUR?

She then signifies her desire to consume two pies with potatoes:

ACUDGOAPERRAPIESWITOTTIES

The damsel disposes of the pies and orders two rolls and cheese.

The waitress brings them and, surveying the young lady's buxom aspect, remarks that it is no wonder she is:

LIKAHOOSESIDE

After the meal the buxom wench would appear to reveal that she is of Oriental extraction. She announces that she is:

BUNGFUNU

Meanwhile, at another table, a small girl is voicing her desire for an ice-cream cornet. Shrilly, she cries:

MAWAWAANTAPOKEYHAT

The child's mother responds by incorporating the desired cornet in a strange threat:

AHLPOKEYHATYE

In another intriguing quirk of the entrancing language heard only in Glasgow, City of Culture, refusal of a desired object often becomes a threat, the desired object being used as a verb. So we have:

AHLBIKEYE or AHLVIDEOCASSETTEYE

IN the evening, the young couple return with the intention of having dinner.

Another perky waitress attends them. She asks:

IZZITDENNERYIREFTER?

The young man confirms he is hungry and could:

DAEWIATIGHTNUR

Then he directs the waitress to bring him the bill of fare:

SEEZAGANDER ATRAMEANYU

The young lady doesn't bother to study the menu card:

HUVYEGOATLASAGNY?

The waitress evidently has not heard of the Continental dish. She seeks enlightenment.

WHITRAHELLZLASAGNY?

Meanwhile the hungry young gent is becoming impatient. He scans the menu and demands to know:

WHERZARAVIOLI?

At once the waitress answers:

SAICINTDOOR OANRALEFTOWERTHERR!

Eventually the customer loses his temper and exclaims:

AWANNI SEERAMANAGER

But he is denied the opportunity of discussing his problems with the person in charge, because as the waitress explains:

IZAWAOOT FURRAMEAL

At The Ballet

A lady paying her first visit to the ballet will be impressed by the ballerina's male partner.

She will express her admiration in two picturesque words:

IDIZNIHAUF WHEECHURABOOT!

The lady's male companion will admire the ballerina, uttering under his breath a couple of complimentary words:

SOMEBOADYOANUR and RERRPERRAPINS

The lady responds to that by declaring that her husband is a:

DURTIAWLDIVVIL

He demands an explanation, saying:

WHIRRAYIGERRINAT?

His wife further alleges that he is showing an unseemly interest in the dancers' nether limbs and rebukes him with:

YURGOGGLINAWA TAWRAELEGS

Once more the gentleman urges his wife to be silent, using the patois phrase:

GIEYURMOOTHAREST

At which point the finale alarms the lady watcher. As she sees the ballerina sink to the floor, she cries:

FELLOANUR SITTIDOON!

The lady's male companion is also puzzled by the proceedings. He asks:

WHISSISAWABOOT?

When she tells him she knows:

HEEHAWABOOTIT

The gentleman ripostes with a favoured solution at any time of crisis:

C'MOAN DOONTIRAPUB

Attending An Avant-Garde Play

THEATRE-GOERS be warned. Not all Glaswegians have been weaned on the classics, on high drama or an avant-garde production.

With the result that you must be prepared to eavesdrop on rather unusual critical reaction:

A lady unhappy with her husband for persuading her to accompany him to a "cult" play will rebuke him harshly with:

DYECARISCULCHUR?

She takes a dislike to the leading actor and, on his second entrance, jeers:

ITSBIGTUMPHIAGAIN

She doesn't understand what the actor is saying:

WHISSIMUMPINABOOT?

Eventually she confesses that the play is beyond her comprehension:

ADOANGERRIT

She declares the production is so boring it could cause one to regurgitate. In the Culture City patois:

TWIDGIEYERABOAK

The husband points out that attending the play is a novel way for his wife to spend the evening. She says:

CHEENGEFAERABINGO

The lady urges her husband to preserve a discreet silence. Her request is made in one picturesque word:

SHUTYURGEGGIE

Her husband points out that they are witnessing an intellectual performance:

WIZEVENOANCHANNELFOWER

The lady now becomes a drama critic and makes an assessment:

SHOORADAMPTCHANCERS

A Day Out At The Zoo

NOWHERE is the picturesque patois heard to greater advantage than at a zoo.

Children visiting the animals demonstrate their linguistic prowess in no small measure.

A small boy catching sight of a bear will point it out to his mother in a charming poetic statement:

HAWMAW ERRABERR!

His mother may ask of him:

WHERRABERR?

By this time, more bears have come into view, and the small boy cries:

ERRAPERRABERRSOWRERR!

The mother, her small son and a woman friend now move on and arrive at the penguins' enclosure.

The mother observes that it is feeding time. The small boy thinks the remark is directed at him and he calls for sustenance:

AHWANNA CHOACLITBISKIT

The mother refuses his request, using the article requested as a verb, thus:

AHLCHOACLITBISKITYE!

As the penguins gulp down the fish from the keeper's hand, the mother tells her friend:

JISLIKEMAMAN

From her friend we once again hear the familiar word:

HOWRAT?

The lady then tells of her husband's prowess in consuming a fish supper. She says that he:

SWALLIZITINAWANUR

At this juncture the ever-observant small boy catches sight of a giraffe. He wants to know:

WHISSATBEASTMAW?

His mother has momentarily forgotten the name of the animal. A diminutive gentleman who is passing tells her:

SAGIRAFFE

The implication that she is ignorant is hotly resented by the lady. She calls after the small man:

GERRAFFYANYAFF AHNUSAGIRAFFE

Eventually the trio finish their tour of the zoo.

Impressed, no doubt, by what he has seen, the small boy addresses his mother with the mysterious word GONNIGEESE.

It turns out to be a plea:

GONNIGEESE ACHOACLITBISKIT?

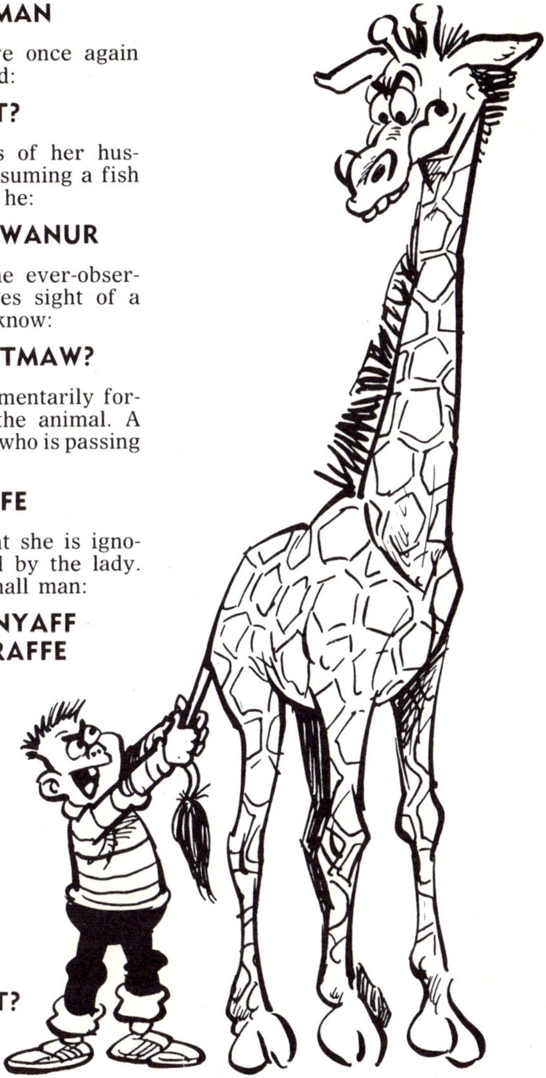

A Sunday Morning At Church

SOME Culture City residents on their way to church on a Sunday morning will use a strange-sounding patois that can baffle visitors.

Let us examine the words and phrases used by Ella and her husband, Sam, as they set out to attend divine service.

Ella espies another couple and, addressing Sam, employs the word:

TAKKADEKKAT

As he quickly scans those around him, she adds:

MATTIMcTATTY

So the complete injunction is:

TAKKADEKKAT MATTIMcTATTY

Sam is still slightly puzzled, to say the least, so he inquires gently:

SUPWIHUR?

Ella elaborates, drawing his attention to the other lady's wide-brimmed hat:

RATHATSHIZGOATOAN

She alleges that the lady imagines herself to be a Princess Diana lookalike:

SHEHINKSHIZRADEIDSPITODI

Sam's summary is succinct and to the point:

DI-ABOLICAL YEMEAN

He is now lagging a step or two behind Ella. She urges him to hurry, using the word GERRA. As in:

GERRAMOOVOAN

At which point Ella notices her husband is limping and gives loud voice to the two unusual rhyming words:

WHITTUR YEHIRPLINFUR?

Sam reveals that his new shoes are compressing his feet. He laments:

MABUNIONZBLEEZIN

Alas, his wife offers him little sympathy. Instead, she wants to know if he has money for the church collection.

Shamefacedly he tells her:

NAWAHHUVNYOANY

And he goes on to explain the reason for this:

FURGOARRIT

Knowing full well that her husband has donated his collection money to his favourite brewery the night before, Ella informs him piously:

YULGOTAERABADFIREYOU

Sam has heard this one before, and the prospect of eternal damnation frightens him not. As he says:

LEASTERSNAE SERMONSDOONRERR

By now they're near the kirk door, and Ella is concerned lest her husband's irreverence is overheard. She whispers:

SHURRITYABAM ERZIELDER

They progress with dignity into the church. Ella greets the elder with the time-honoured phrase:

YURLOOKINWEEL HUVYEBINSEEK?

They pause inside the door as Ella's mind suddenly casts back to their rather hurried breakfast. She inquires of Sam:

JOOTURNAFFRAGAS?

Sam looks vacantly at his beloved before replying:

NAWJOONO?

The lady, furious, turns and begins to retrace her steps. Sam asks:

WHERRURYEGAUN?

Promptly comes the conclusive comment:

WURGAUNHAME

Driving On The Streets Of Glasgow

A visitor to the City of Culture may be given a lift in a car driven by a native Glaswegian.

In which case he or she will be able to study the words and phrases used when a true Glaswegian is driving in the city.

Perhaps the word most frequently heard is GITOOTRA.

It is used in conjunction with other words. So we hear the impatient driver calling to a slow driver:

GITOOTRAROADYACRAWLUR

Caught up in a lengthy tail-back, the driver will lament:

WE'LL NIVVER GITOOTRAQUEUE THEDAY

The word GITOOTRA is also heard when a tyre is flat:

AHLHUVTI GITOOTRA SPERRWHEEL

And if smoke suddenly erupts from the radiator, the passenger is told:

GITOOTRA CAURKWIK!

The driver of a car who has almost caused a collision will be told:

GITOOTRATBANGER TAEAHBELTYE

A car swerving sharply in front of the driver might cause him to react thus:

YAMUG YURBEVVIED

On discovering the true cause of the erratic driving, he may reveal the full extent of his chauvinistic tendencies:

AHMIGHTAKNEW ADAMPTWUMMANDRIVER

And he may add:

SHELEARNTAEDRIVE PUSHINAPRAM

The driver of a bus that comes too close will meet with the plea:

PLAYRAGEMMEMAC

Caught in a traffic jam, the Glaswegian at the wheel may tell his passenger in a single word:

YILHUVTIHOOFIT

IF however, the driver finds himself free of traffic, he will want to make up time:

ALHUVTI PITRAFITDOON

This will not endear him to the local constabulary. Glancing in his mirror, he may exclaim:

AWNAWITZAPOLISCAUR

Pulled over to the kerb and asked to explain his speed, he may offer a variety of responses:

MASPEEDOSBROKE or AMADOACTUR

Parking is another problem. If your driver finds a space he will inform other drivers, with the words:

ERRASPACE! ATSMASPACE! GETYERAIN SPACEPAL!

There are, however, areas of town where he might prefer not to park, because:

RANEDSULHUVMAWHEELSAFF

The city has its own urban motorway, which is often subject to repair. Your driver will let you know of approaching roadworks thus:

AWNAWMERRCONES!

At the filling station he will show his concern for the environment by announcing his intention to fill up with:

YONGREENJUICE

And when paying for his unleaded petrol he will request his free gift with the words:

GOATONYTUMBLERS?

Back home after his journey, his car might be a mite dusty. His wife might comment:

RAMOTURSMANKY!

If You're Invited To A Wedding

ONE'S enjoyment and appreciation of the ceremony and celebration could easily be spoiled by not being fully conversant with the nuptial patois.

HURMURRA

Is, of course, the accepted term for the mother of the bride.

Rating equally highly on the social scale is:

UROLLMAN

Whose vital role as father of the bride is to lead the bride up the aisle.

First indication that the big moment has arrived will be when spectators whisper excitedly:

RAMO'ORS ATTRADOOR

Thereby revealing to all and sundry that the wedding car has arrived:

ERRSADIE NU!

Indicates that the bride, Sadie, has stepped from the limousine.

Inside the church guests will be making shrewd observations and assessments:

ZATRAMUG?

Is how a guest who hasn't yet met the bridegroom will make a gentle enquiry as to the identity of the gentleman to whom Sadie is being married.

Having had confirmation, the immediate reaction might be:

ZOFFIWEE!

Indicating that the bridegroom's stature is somewhat unremarkable.

If the ceremony is performed satisfactorily, both families will no doubt concur:

TWENTAFF NOBAD

ON then to the reception. It's only a matter of time before the outsider will have to interpret such classics as:

SHIZZAGUID HOFFINUR

A reference to a lady guest who has perhaps been imbibing too freely.

Exactly how much the majority of the guests drink will depend on:

AWHIPROON FURRAKITTY

A quaint custom that ensures the cost of providing refreshments is shared equally.

The announcement that the wedding breakfast is served, and that guests can now partake of the feast will be greeted with delight:

NOOFURRA TIGHTNUR

Everyone can now relax and enjoy the more social side of the afternoon.

And so the celebrations continue unremittingly.

UROLLMAN'S UNNERATABLE

The bride's father is resting after refreshments.

GONNYGEEZ YERSANGSAM?

Will the bride's uncle give us his rendering of "Nobody's Child?"

SAMZAWFFY PEELLYWALLY

The bride's Uncle Sam is overcome by emotion.

GERRIMOOTKWIK

Conduct him speedily to an ante-room.

SUSIESWENTANSKAILTA PINTOWRURSEL

Susan, the bridesmaid, has inadvertently spilled some of her boyfriend's refreshment over herself.

The lively celebrations end when the bride and bridegroom bid their guests farewell:

WARRAFTY TROON FURWURHONEYMOON

Thereby revealing to all and sundry that they the happy couple intend having a few bracing days to themselves on the Ayrshire coast.

A Seat At The Cinema

A night at the cinema will make a pleasant, relaxing change for visitors.

Enchanting words and phrases come from speakers of the Culture City language when they are at "the picturs".

A damsel will remark to her male escort:

SARERRFILLUMINTIT?

Then, moved by the drama on the screen she will confess:

AHMNEARGREETINSOAHUM

Her escort will then make the oft-used request:

BEYURAGE

The star of the film impresses the young lady. She sighs:

WHIRRADISH

Her escort preserves a glum silence. His fair companion wants his verdict on the film star:

DEIDHUNKY INTY?

Her boy friend is not so enthusiastic, and implies that the film star lacks masculinity. He conveys this opinion with the word:

BIGJENNIWULLOX

The young lady praises the female star of the film, saying:

SHIZLUVLISOSHEIZ

Her escort is less than enthusiastic. He admits:

SHIZNOBAD

Later the damsel is far from pleased when the young man dismisses the film drama as:

ALOADACOADSWALLUP

OLDER cinemagoers are even more critical of what they see on the screen.

Love scenes are apt to annoy the middle-aged lady. An amorous encounter between the male and female stars may bring forth the condemnatory comment:

RATWIDSEECKINYE

As the male advances to kiss the female star, the Culture City lady is alarmed and declares that it looks as if he is going to:

BITERADIALAFFUR

She contends that the love scene could cause her to regurgitate. She uses the phrase:

TWID GIEYERABOAK

She also disapproves of the male star in the film. Her husband reminds her that their daughter admires him:

OORJENNYSEZHEZAHERTTHROAB

His wife reacts to this with a loud:

HUH! THELASSIZNOOADAYS!

The husband points out that she idolised Clark Gable. His wife asserts:

WORTHHAUFADIZZENOTHATWEESSKELF

As they emerge from the cinema, she gives the film her succinct verdict:

MONEYDOONRADRAIN

Saturday Night Fever . . .

THE younger set will probably head for discos to dance the nights away.

Even there, they will come across some bewildering conversations:

A young man, noticing the absence of another young gent's partner, will inquire:

WHERRSYURLUMBUR?

He will be informed that the damsel has returned to the ladies' room to apply some make-up. The full reply is:

SHIZPITTINOANURFACE

A gentleman wishing to dance with a young lady will express his request in two words:

FANCIA WRIGGLEROON?

If the maiden is fatigued, she will utter the one trenchant word :

NAWAMWABBIT

One young lady, Sadie, tells another damsel, Nellie, that she has espied a mutual friend. She asks:

ZATURMANJEANSWI BIRAWAY?

To which Nellie will reply:

AYE ZOFFIAULLUKKIN INTI?

Whereupon Sadie discloses the reason for the gentleman's venerable appearance:

RATMIDDEN WIDPITYEARS OANONYGUY

But Sadie is impressed by the gentleman's terpsichorean gyrations. She declares that he can:

FERRLITWISTISBOADIABOOT

Nellie reveals:

AYE EZARICHTAWLTWISTER

She might go on to explain that disco-dancing till 3 am has taxed her strength, declaring:

ITAKSITOOTAYI

So she eventually decides to go home and informs her would-be partner:

AMFURAFF

Which prompts Sadie to inquire of her friend:

GOATRATIMEOANYE?

When told it is after 3 am, she emits a cry of alarm and laments:

MAMURRALGIEMELALDI!

So she makes one last request to Nellie:

SEEZALENIACOUPLAQUID

Nellie asks:

WHITFUR?

And Sadie explains that her pedal extremities have become painful. In fact, she claims:

MAFEETSHINGINAFFME

Which is why she cannot walk home. To explain this fully she uses the AHLHUVTAE technique:

AHLHUVTAETAKKATAXI

On Meeting People From Edinburgh

THERE has long been a mild rivalry between Edinburgh or, to give it its Glescaese name, Embra.

This is illustrated when Greta from the Gorbals is quizzed by her friend Teenie about a couple from the Capital she met who were visiting the Culture City.

"Ah heard them talking'," says Teenie, "Ur they furriners?" Greta replies:

AYE THURFAEEMBRA

Teenie remarks that the Edinburgh couple have a:

FUNNIWEYOTOKKIN

Greta agrees that their speech pattern is:

PANLOAF or BOOLINRAMOOTH

Teenie is curious to know:

WHITTUREYHEREFUR?

It appears the Edinburgh couple have come to Glasgow to attend a concert featuring the works of Bartok.

But Greta is under a misapprehension and tells Teenie that the Edinburgh lady:

WAANTSTIHEAR BARTALK

Greta goes on to say she directed the visitors to her favourite hostelry, as it is:

ARERRPUBFURRAPATTUR

A week later Greta encounters the Edinburgh couple for the second time and says:

NOAWAHAMEYIT?

The lady tells her that she and her husband are leaving the next day as they don't want to miss the start of the Edinburgh Festival.

Greta tells her that she once attended that feast of culture. Asked if she enjoyed it she declares:

TWIZ PUREMURDUR

And she goes on to say:

EMBRAWIZ FUAWIDBEEZ

And that she was:

BOREDOOTMASKULL

Nettled by this, the Edinburgh gentleman intervenes to say it wasn't unexpected that a keelie from Glasgow would not appreciate the wonderful Edinburgh Festival.

Greta is furious and screeches:

OHUMMAKEELIEUMMA?

The Glasgow lady then gives him some advice:

GITBACKTAEEMBRA YANYAFF

Adding two sinister words:

AFOREYEGIT MAFITUPYURJAXI

Glaswegians tend not to think too much of the capital's monuments and traditions, either. Consider their views on Princes Street:

NAEMAIRNAGAIRDENPATH

Or The Castle:

RAGORBALSOANAHILL

Arthur's Seat:

LIKAGREENPLOOK

Greyfriar's Bobby:

YONDUGWIZZAHEIDBANGER

The Scott Monument:

SNOFEENISHEDYIT

Murrayfield:

AGIDPLACEFURCOOS

At A Football Match

IT will be impossible for visitors to the European City of Culture not to be caught up in one way or another with the enthusiasm that abounds when the subject of silky soccer crops up.

Whether they take in an international football match at Hampden Park or a kickabout in a public park, they will benefit from tackling this introduction to the terminology of the terracing:

As the teams warm up on the field, the enthusiast will join those around him in the singing of what might sound similar to an aboriginal tribal chant. In other words, the Earwig Song:

EARWIG-O! EARWIG-O! EARWIG-O!

Further cries of encouragement will soon sound round the ground:

GETOARIN or GETTINTAETHUM

Interspersed with joyful cries of:

WEARRAPEEPUL

As the game ebbs and flows, a whole variety of emotions will manifest themselves through the following expressions:

SHOOTYAPOLTIS

Which is stern advice to a player who has beaten three opponents in the penalty box but then turns to repeat the performance.

AWANPITYERFROAKOAN

A suggestion that one of the players is playing like what is commonly described as "a big Jessie"!

YAWEEIDJIT

Diminutive wingers who consistently make errors are frequently referred to as such.

ZATNOSEECKNIN?

A general expression of disenchantment. Can refer equally well to the performance of players in either team, the referee, the linesmen, the weather or the fact the tea-room has run out of meat delicacies.

YOU will hear GIEMA used in many different ways by supporters who disagree with the referee's decision:

GIEMAPERRASPECS

Which is a suggestion that the match controller perhaps needs to fork out the cost of a visit to an optomotrist.

Failure by the same official to notice illegal play by the opposition will solicit the directive:

OPENYUREENREF

Righteous indignation usually accompanies a spate of SNOAS:

SNOAKOARNUR, SNOAGOAL

These are common terms which signify the caller does not concur with the assessment of the match officials.

If, however, he feels the officials would appreciate his opinion, he will advise them that one of the opposing players has inadvertently run the ball over the side-line with the time-honoured plea:

SASHIE!

Another word used frequently is GITTIM, as in:

GITTIMAFF

Which usually suggests that the team's performance might be improved if one particular individual was replaced by a substitute.

If, on the other hand, the enthusiast feels the recurring transgressions of the opposing centre-back merit dismissal, he will urge:

RIDCAIRD RARUDDIBAMPOAT

Towards the end of the encounter, depending on the state of the game, whole sections of the stadium might echo to:

AMAWAFURRAHAUFANAHAUF

Indicating that of the 50,000 individuals present, certain of them are preparing to consume either a celebratory or consolatory refreshment.

Settling Down To Watch TV

THE pilgrim to the epicentre of culture on the banks of the Clyde may be invited to the home of one of the inhabitants.

If so, the visitor will be fascinated by the subtle nuances of the language spoken by the natives, especially when the TV set is switched on.

The lady of the house addresses her young son with an imperious cry of:

TURNRATRACKITAFF

The boy defies her and receives a stern warning:

SASKELPOANRALUGYULGET!

Still the youngster refuses to switch off the pop concert. He makes an anguished protest, saying that two young gents whose artistry he admires are next on the programme:

AWNAWMAW!

And he adds:

BROSIZOANIXT

The two young gents known as Bros sing a number, then they are followed by a somewhat noisy group.

From the mother comes a stern command to her son:

ANUFFARAT

The boy switches to BBC 1. This time the man of the house reacts violently. He cries:

SWOGANAGAIN!

He adds that the Irish chat show host is:

NIVVERAFF

The wife declares that she admires Mr Wogan, saying:

AHINKEEZMAAGIC

She praises the Irishman:

EEZAYERATHAPPY

With a certain cynicism in his voice, the husband says:

NAEWUNNER EEZPEYEDFORTYTHOOSANTAYEAR

The Wogan programme is switched off and the family find themselves watching what is billed as a "black comedy".

After failing to understand the dialogue, the lady of the house protests:

RISIZDIRE!

Her husband agrees. He too is puzzled and admits:

AHDOANGERRIT

Soon the TV set is tuned to another channel. This time the screen is occupied by a loud-voiced "alternative comedian".

His outpourings are not relished by the Culture City family. The husband declares the comedian is as:

FUNNIASAGUMBOIL

THE eldest child is sitting O grades and would like to watch Channel Four. Her father declines, saying:

AWRATARTYSTUFF GUZOWERMAHEID

Mother is quick to the defence of her daughter, telling her husband that:

POSMINPAT GUZOWERYURHEID

In the face of feminine logic, father switches to Channel Four, which is showing a documentary on Culture City. He cries:

HAWERZMAMAMMIESHOOSE

Recognition of the maternal abode stirs the family to a pitch of excitement, which increases when a neighbour is spotted in a street scene, encouraging mother to exclaim:

SWEESAMMYNARGYLESTREET!

But excitement turns to envy when Wee Sammy, a street entertainer, is subsequently interviewed about the renaissance of his home town. Father comments:

WITZATWEENUMPTY NOBOOTKULCHUR?

In disgust he changes channels again, and the family find themselves watching Rab C. Nesbitt. Father is triumphant:

NOORATSKULCHUR!

Bringing In The New Year

THE City of Culture celebrations will last well beyond the summer.

Perhaps even into the New Year. Which means visitors could well find themselves in the midst of traditional Hogmanay celebrations.

They will be well advised to study these words and phrases used as the natives observe the ancient rites.

GUIDNOO YEARTYI

I wish you a good New Year.

SAMETIYOU

I reciprocate your good wishes.

ANMONEYORUM

May you have many prosperous years.

SEEZADAUDABLACKBUN

I wish to partake of the traditional Hogmanay delicacy.

RAULGANNETSETTIT

My mother-in-law has consumed it all.

WHERRAKERRYOOT?

Where are the essential first-footing supplies?

DAMPBAMPOT DRAPTIT

The confounded fool has dropped the package of supplies.

WHIRRAKERRYOAN

What shocking behaviour!

NO doubt some of the visitors will also be puzzled by sundry remarks made to and about celebrants by their wives:

LAYAFFRABIDDI

Cease sampling that non-vintage wine.

YEKANNIHODDIT

Your capacity for refreshments is lamentably poor.

YUVHUDDANUFF

Your Ne'erday revels are at an end.

EZFELLOANAFLERR

The power has departed from his legs.

Which usually precedes a flurry of SHUVVIMINRAS:

SHUVVIMINRA TAXI or SHUVVIMINRA BED.

THE happy cries of Ne'erday party-goers are often charmingly picturesque:

FURRASHUFFUL?

Would you care to dance?

GEESAWEECHEEPUR

Permit me to salute you with a chaste kiss.

HAUNZAFFRAMUTTON

I do not wish to be embraced by you.

Finally, many Scots will reminisce about their jolly revels, using such terms as:

WHIRRAHEIDAHUV

My cranium is throbbing.

YURNOSOBERYIT

I detect a woolly aspect in your demeanour.

AVANOFFISERRKYTE

Black bun, scampi, and ginger wine do not mix.

HEZAFFTYIZFLEAPIT

He wishes to experience the healing power of slumber.

But the phrase most often heard at this time of year is, of course, that poignant cry:

ORRABESTIYIZAW!

At The Burrell

THE first inkling Glaswegians had that they were cultured was when Sir William Burrell's collection of objets d'art was put on display in a South-Side park.

Since then, the Burrell Collection has become a magnet for tourists. Many families make it a Sunday outing—families such as Shug and Ina McSwally, with their children, Brett and Fallon.

The McSwallys drive into the leafy glades of Pollok Estate. Young Fallon is unaccustomed to profuse greenery and inquires why there's so much of it round about her. Her mother explains:

SKOZITZAPARKPET

Brett is looking forward to some fun and is curious to know:

WERZISHOOTANISWINGS?

Father tells his son it is not that kind of park:

ZNAESWINGS—SAWART

Entering the Collection by its Gothic portals, their attention is drawn to a magnificent Greek bowl. Shug is moved to wonder:

HOOJIGERRATUNNERABED?

Ina reveals Lord Elgin's treasure is not a chamber pot, then catches sight of Brett fingering the Chinese porcelain. She warns him to:

LAVERAYORNYMENTSALANE

She needn't have worried. One of the attendants has already spotted the danger and admonished the lad:

VAKACHYAGAIN YILGITRAJILE

The McSwallys find themselves in a room hung with medieval tapestries. Examining a hunting scene, Ina comments:

SARERRBITACAIRPIT

But Fallon is puzzled:

WITZITOANAWAFUR?

Shug explains:

SOZWEENYAFFSLIKYOUL NOSTAUNOANIT

The family proceeds around the Collection, eventually confronting Rodin's sculpture, The Thinker. Fallon is transfixed, but her mother is horrified, and leads the family swiftly from the premises, declaring she did not want them clapping eyes on:

SCUDDIEMEN!